Color of Love

A Topical Study on Christlikeness
and Racial Reconciliation

Leader Discussion Guide

Contents

Using this Curriculum

Dear Leader,

Greetings and thank you for choosing to lead this study within your church family! We deeply believe these words, the discussions you and your group will have, and the corresponding prayer times will have lasting impacts on the group members, your church fellowship, and your communities.

As a way of introduction and preparation, please read the corresponding "About this Study" section at the beginning of the Participant Book. Below, you will find instructions and information for using this curriculum.

We have designed this study for a small group environment meeting for eight consecutive weeks. It includes two primary components: the Participant Book which gives Biblical context and thoughtful preparation for the group meeting times, and this Leader Discussion Guide. Each leader and group participant will need a copy of the Participant Book, but only the group leader(s) will need a copy of the Discussion Guide. Each week, group members should read the corresponding chapter prior to the group meeting time in preparation for the discussion. Both Participant and Leader components are essential to this study as they are intimately linked with each other in scope and topic, and the content of each brings depth that would be missed without the other.

The Participant Book is the foundation for this study. As such, it is the primary "landing pad" for all discussion within the group. This text focuses heavily on what Scripture teaches in the conversation of racial reconciliation, and is therefore the main reading source utilized.

This Discussion Guide is designed to help you, the group leader, facilitate the weekly group discussions that follow up the reading for each chapter. You will find several components to facilitate the flow of the meeting: Scripture, History, Terminology, Discussion Questions, and Prayer. Each of these sections are titled and filled with content to develop a flow of conversation in your group.

The Discussion Guide intentionally brings attention to specific societal events in our nation's history. The discussion of reconciliation in America cannot move forward without learning and acknowledging the history and realities of our national racial make-up. We want to include these topics in our discussion time as an opportunity for people to converse and hear perspectives and opinions within the group that may be different than their own. This is a valuable part of loving someone well even if he/she may think differently than you.

As it relates to the group discussion times, please take note of the following practical suggestions and overviews for each discussion element. First, video links are offered in this Guide for multiple group discussion times. If possible, proper audio/video technology should be utilized. Second, this Discussion Guide includes a handful of internet links to aid you in gaining general knowledge regarding specific topics. These websites are meant to be tools for you in beginning your study and understanding of racial history in America. These are not meant to be exhaustive. You are encouraged to explore other information sources as well.

SCRIPTURE

Because God's Word is the foundation of all truth, we begin every group meeting with a passage of Scripture. All the Scriptures written in the Discussion Guide are meant to be read aloud and then discussed in the group setting. The questions that follow ask the participants to stop and acknowledge what God's Word actually says. While it may feel redundant to ask group members to speak out obvious information, this process aids in enabling minds and hearts to more fully grasp the concepts presented in each offered passage.

HISTORY and TERMINOLOGY

The history and terminology sections are meant to give tangible, factual information regarding racism in America. As a leader, please make sure you are familiar enough with the topics to discuss them, ensuring that you communicate accurate information to your group.

Depending on the length of your meeting times, these sections can be overwhelming. Please remember that the ideas and information in these sections are critical for understanding why and where we are as a nation and in the Church in regards to racial reconciliation. Open the discussion and give good definitions, but this section is designed to simply BEGIN the conversation. Don't feel the need to plumb the depths of these topics or solve all the injustices. Encourage group members to continue their own study of these topics.

In light of that, leaders are highly encouraged to read, pray, and prepare thoroughly ahead of group meeting times. If at all possible, please choose and read two of the books listed in the suggested reading (found at the end of the chapters in the Participant Book) for your own preparation for leading this group. If you are new to the reconciliation conversation, this will go a long way in helping you form your own thoughts prior to leading others through this course. Also, please pre-view all links and materials you plan to share with your group. We have included options we have found helpful in this guide.

DISCUSSION QUESTIONS

These questions are designed to try to synthesize thoughts and ideas from both the Participant Book and the discussion. These questions attempt to bring home main ideas, reveal any areas that require a change of heart or mind, and begin to give ideas for next steps.

If you find that you are running out of time (making sure you leave time for the last element - explained below), these questions can also be used as homework, or in a follow-up group email. However, moving through the discussion elements with intention and timeliness helps to ensure good discussion around these ideas as well.

PRAYER

Lastly, we have found that prayer is vital and binding. This is maybe the most valuable part of the group meeting time. The true work of reconciliation cannot be done without the working of the Holy Spirit in the minds and lives of people submitted to the Lord, and as such our best vehicle for seeing His work accomplished starts with prayer. In addition, spending time in prayer together as a group binds people together in deep ways.

An easy way to facilitate this is to communicate clearly with your group that you will be holding a time of prayer at the end, that a Scripture will be read/made available, and while you will open the prayer time, all group members are encouraged to also pray aloud around ideas presented in the Scripture. Depending on the comfort level of the group members, this could feel challenging at first. We encourage you to not let a challenge discourage you. Do not neglect this time of prayer. Prioritize it. And while it may be uncomfortable at first, set the expectation and leave room for various participants to pray out loud as well.

Again, this conversation is beautiful and necessary for the body of Christ. Thank you for being willing to serve through leading these discussion times. Our prayer for you and your group is that the needed fruit of reconciliation, borne by the Holy Spirit, will be made evident in these conversations and in the relationships that will be built.

Samuel & Brandy Knopp

Week 1: Introduction

SCRIPTURE

Ephesians 2:13-15, NASB

But now in Christ Jesus you who formerly were far off have been brought near by the blood of Christ. For He Himself is our peace, who made both groups into one and broke down the barrier of the dividing wall, by abolishing in His flesh the enmity, which is the Law of commandments contained in ordinances, so that in Himself He might make the two into one new man, thus establishing peace, and might reconcile them both in one body to God through the cross, by it having put to death the enmity.

What ideas do you see represented in this Scripture?

- Who is our peace?
- Who establishes peace?
- Who makes two groups into one?

- Who abolishes enmity?
- Who breaks down dividing walls?
- How is reconciliation accomplished?

In this study, we recognize and glorify even that the solution to our problems is found in Jesus. We must individually and corporately be rightly related to Jesus in order to see peace come about on the earth. This is not a passive thought saying Jesus will make all things right upon His return. It is an active joining in to a right personal understanding that Jesus transforms us, His followers, and moves us to engage rightly with the people around us.

HISTORY

Present a high level overview of African American history in the US.
In the group context, there will not be enough time to discuss all of these events in detail. We suggest that you present this list of historical topics and ask people to identify any references they are not familiar with. Then allow another group member to try to briefly give an explanation.

The purpose of this activity is to bring historical events "forward" that are often more unfamiliar to white members but very formative for black members. Our joint history, good or bad, shapes our cultural moment now. This discussion can give context for much of the conversation going forward. Be sure to invite group members to utilize the many educational options available to them for further understanding of any of these historical events.

https://www.history.com/topics/black-history/black-history-milestones
If, as the group leader, you are not familiar with or comfortable speaking generally about any of the topics below, please consider reading/watching the article above and doing some preparation work beforehand. This is a very high level look at the racial history in America.

The historical topics below present context for how we've come to where we are today in the US regarding race:

- Slave trade
- 3/5 Compromise (US Constitution)
- Civil War
- Reconstruction
- Separate but equal
- KKK
- Lynchings

- Destruction of Black Wall Street in Tulsa, OK
- Jim Crow laws
- Desegregation
- Civil Rights Movement
- Affirmative Action
- War on Drugs
- Barack Obama/ Kamala Harris

TERMINOLOGY

"Imago Dei"

This term is Latin for "image of God." The concept of being "image bearers" comes up repeatedly in the Participant Book (pg 1, 3). Ask group members to define "imago Dei" and then describe who this term applies to and why. This discussion should lead to the reality that all humans regardless of race and belief system are image bearers, and that we all have worth and value in the eyes of God.

DISCUSSION QUESTIONS

• Explain racism as a human construct (Participant Book, pg 3).

• What ways has the church NOT been a credible witness in regards to racism in America? What ways HAS the church been a credible witness?

• Let's dream: what would a reconciled church look like?

PRAYER

Psalm 17:15 (Participant Book, pg 5)
As for me, I will see Your face in righteousness;
I shall be satisfied when I awake in Your likeness.

Isaiah 26: 8b-9
The desire of our soul is for Your name
And for the remembrance of You.
With my soul I have desired You in the night,
Yes, by my spirit within me I will seek You early;
For when Your judgments are in the earth,
The inhabitants of the world will learn righteousness.

Father, the desire of our souls is for Your name and for the remembrance of You. The desire of our hearts is that we would look like You, think like You, act like You in the earth. Open our eyes to see Your ways, Your judgments in the earth. Help us to seek You with any time we may have. And help us to join with You and Your judgments that bring righteousness in the earth. Amen.

Week 2: Care

Colossians 3:12-17, NASB (Participant Book, pg 11)

So, as those who have been chosen of God, holy and beloved, put on a heart of compassion, kindness, humility, gentleness and patience; bearing with one another, and forgiving each other, whoever has a complaint against anyone; just as the Lord forgave you, so also should you. Beyond all these things put on love, which is the perfect bond of unity. Let the peace of Christ rule in your hearts, to which indeed you were called in one body; and be thankful. Let the word of Christ richly dwell within you, with all wisdom teaching and admonishing one another with psalms and hymns and spiritual songs, singing with thankfulness in your hearts to God. Whatever you do in word or deed, do all in the name of the Lord Jesus, giving thanks through Him to God the Father.

What are the verbs (actions asked of a believer) in this Scripture?
- Put on a heart of…
- Bear with one another…forgive one another…
- Put on love...
- Let the peace of Christ rule in your hearts...
- Let the word of Christ richly dwell within you…

Describe a time when you have seen actions presented in this Scripture used towards you.

Describe a time when you have seen actions presented in this Scripture used transracially.

HISTORY

Caring for someone else often hinges on even knowing there is a problem that needs care or attention. That means it is critical for brothers and sisters in Christ to be aware of the lived experiences of others around them.

If appropriate technology is available, consider showing the following video of Phil Vischer, founding member of Veggie Tales and leading voice in the kids program "What's In the Bible" as he explains the history of racism in America. https://www.youtube.com/watch?v=AGUwcs9qJXY (approx 17mins)

If the technology for viewing this video is not available, compile statistics on some of the current difficulties facing many of our racially diverse brothers and sisters such as mass incarceration, wealth gap, police brutality, or inequalities in education. Many of the suggested reading texts from the Participant Book speak broadly to these issues as well.

TERMINOLOGY
....

"Proximate to a need"

This is a phrase that is used in the realm of societal justice to mean a multi-step process that results in an action. First, a person must recognize a need around them. Second, a person must care enough about that need to initiate a response. Third, a person must take steps to get close to that need with the intention to learn more and/or respond with help - like the Good Samaritan. (Participant Book, pg 7-8)

The challenge here is for group members to mentally look over their own spheres of influence, see what needs are presented to them, and consider ways they can step in to help meet a need.

DISCUSSION QUESTIONS
....

- How would you measure your level of awareness specifically related to the current realities of racial disparity?

- Describe what "caring" for someone of another ethnicity might look like.

- Are you aware of any needs in your sphere of influence that you could learn more about or respond to?

PRAYER

....

1 Corinthians 13:4-7, NASB (Participant Book, pg 10)
Love is patient, love is kind and is not jealous; love does not brag and is not arrogant, does not act unbecomingly; it does not seek its own, is not provoked, does not take into account a wrong suffered, does not rejoice in unrighteousness, but rejoices with the truth; bears all things, believes all things, hopes all things, endures all things.

Father, we humbly come before you confessing we want to love others well, but know we daily fall short of this in so many areas of relationships. Forgive us for not treating other image bearers with the love and dignity they deserve as fellow children of God. Father, give us the desire and ability to lift our eyes from our own circumstances and to actually see the people around us with Your eyes and Your heart. And Father, as we engage our eyes, change our minds and hearts to care enough to move toward others in love and acts of service.

Week 3: Humility

SCRIPTURE

Philippians 2:1-5, NASB (Participant Book, pg 15)

Therefore if there is any encouragement in Christ, if there is any consolation of love, if there is any fellowship of the Spirit, if any affection and compassion, make my joy complete by being of the same mind, maintaining the same love, united in spirit, intent on one purpose. Do nothing from selfishness or empty conceit, but with humility of mind regard one another as more important than yourselves; do not merely look out for your own personal interests, but also for the interests of others. Have this attitude in yourselves which was also in Christ Jesus…

What actions, behaviors, ideas, etc., should be produced in people who claim Jesus as their Lord and Savior? (doing nothing out of selfishness or deceit; being unified in mind, love and spirit; not looking out for oneself only, regarding others as more important than themselves)

What are the motivations of the believers who act in these ways? (the fellowship of the Spirit, affection and compassion, love)

With those attributes in mind, throw out some ideas on how believers can respond to each other across racial lines.

HISTORY

We have discussed, in part, our nation's history and the effects of particular policies in creating racial disparity. Today we will talk about something a little uncomfortable and sometimes hard to wrap our minds around. We want to talk about the complicity of the church in racial disunity. How has the church added to the disunity we see in our world today?

Introduce history of how and why black churches began in America. A simple wikipedia search brings up a basic launch pad of historical information on this topic:
https://en.wikipedia.org/wiki/
Black_Church_(African_American)#:~:text=In%201787%20in%20Philadelphia%2
C%20the,formed%20the%20Free%20African%20Society.

Ask the group if they are aware of any other ways in which the American church has been complicit in or complacent regarding the disunity we see in our nation. Some quick discussion options are the open door many churches offered to the KKK and the prohibition of interracial marriages.

TERMINOLOGY

"Privilege Walk"

Numerous companies, social groups, sports clubs, and schools use a "privilege walk" as a tool to show the participants the various differences and disparities between two different groups. In relation to the conversation on race, for example, the leader will ask all participants to line up side by side equally on one side of the room with the instructions to take a step forward each time a following statement is true for their personal life. Economic, social, educational, and opportunity differences are easily seen as particular members are able to "advance" across the room and others are not able.

Below is a powerful option presenting a video of a high school group performing a privilege walk. Debrief and ask for responses after if time allows.
Video example:
https://www.youtube.com/watch?v=4K5fbQ1-zps (5 min video)

Explaining/demonstrating a privilege walk gives a more tangible example of differences between lived experiences. This is a great tool to help group members see and understand perspectives beyond their own. Please preview the explanation document before the meeting time. While it is unlikely that there will be enough time in this meeting to do a privilege walk as a group, it is helpful to read through the questions to gain a deeper understanding of this activity.
Explanation:
http://doloreshuerta.org/wp-content/uploads/2020/04/privilege-walk.pdf

DISCUSSION QUESTIONS

- Recognizing elements that constitute "white culture" can be challenging since much of "white culture" is also considered normal American culture. But recognizing the fact that white people have ways that can be described as "white" and not just "normal" is an eye opening exercise. Can anyone give an example of something that would be considered part of "white culture"? (Participant Book, pg 13)

- Thinking specifically about engaging with people of another ethnicity other than your own, what are some ways we can walk in humility and/or demonstrate humility?

- Do you have any ideas on how your church can cross racial barriers to become more multi-ethnic?

PRAYER

Romans 15:5-7

Now may the God of patience and comfort grant you to be like-minded toward one another, according to Jesus Christ, that you may with one mind and one mouth glorify the God and Father of our Lord Jesus Christ.

Father, we take a moment today to thank You. We thank You for loving us enough to give us an example of what humility looks like. Thank You for sending Your Son not only for our salvation and propitiation for our sin but also as a demonstration and example for us to follow. Father, we desire to see Your hope and truth made manifest in the world around us. Enable and embolden us, Your people, to walk in humility one with another and thus also be demonstrators of Your truth, light, and hope.

Week 4: Repentance

SCRIPTURE

2 Chronicles 7:14 (Participant Book, pg 18)
If My people who are called by My name will humble themselves, and pray and seek My face, and turn from their wicked ways, then I will hear from heaven, and will forgive their sin and heal their land.

What are the actions of repentance outlined in this verse? (being called by God's name, humbling of self, prayer, seeking the face of God, and turning from wicked ways)

What is God's promise in response to this kind of repentance?

According to this Scripture, is God's response only for individuals?

HISTORY

Instead of focusing on America's racial history this week, let's take a closer look at some Biblical history. The following are just a few examples where God's people recognized their need for and/or were called to corporate repentance (Participant Book, pg 21):

- Judges 10:10-16: the people repent for serving foreign gods
- Joel 2:12-17: a call to fast and pray in response to a locust plague that had devastated the land and another one forthcoming
- Jeremiah 14:1-9: repentance in response to drought
- Daniel 9:3-19: Daniel repents and intercedes for the nation in exile

Either familiarize yourself with these passages to be able to speak to them or choose two for the group to read aloud. Then begin a discussion highlighting the Biblical precedent for corporate and personal repentance.

TERMINOLOGY

"Reconciliation"

While this seems like an obvious term with obvious meaning, take a moment to define it technically, and discuss what reconciliation can/should look like in real life and real time.

A dictionary definition of reconciliation is: "the restoration of friendly relations" or "the action of making one view or belief compatible with another."[1]

Obviously, we don't want reconciliation to be a platform in which the truth of the Gospel is compromised. But, is it possible for two people to experience two different life circumstances, develop different preferences, have different family and societal histories, etc., and still walk in unity and reconciliation? Absolutely!

One of the challenges in reconciliation is the rebuilding of trust. As mentioned in this week's chapter (Participant Book, pg 18), think about reconciliation between a husband and wife when hurts, wounds, and sins have taken place. Repentance and forgiveness are the absolute first and necessary steps. But as our title Scripture indicates, a turning away from wicked ways has to also take place. Trust has to be restored. And that takes place when the offender walks in humility, truth, and love in a repeated manner, showing a changed heart and life over and over and over again. Reconciliation takes time and commitment. It takes intentionally working to build trust and relationship, showing over and over again that past sins are not part of the present and will not be carried into the future.

DISCUSSION QUESTIONS

- Wrestling with the concepts of corporate sin in America, what arenas of injustice has the Church taken a stand for?

- In what ways has the Church engaged in a more corporate acknowledgement of guilt and wrong on behalf of the nation?

- Why do you think there has been push back to not accept racial injustice with the same treatment?

---

[1] Google, https://www.google.com/search?
q=def+reconciliation&rlz=1C1GCEA_enUS797US800&oq=def&aqs=chrome.0.69i59j69i57j69i59j0j69i65j69i60l3.1857j0j7&sourceid
=chrome&ie=UTF-8&safe=active&ssui=on

PRAYER

2 Corinthians 7:9-10, NASB

I now rejoice, not that you were made sorrowful, but that you were made sorrowful to the point of repentance; for you were made sorrowful according to the will of God, so that you might not suffer loss in anything through us. For the sorrow that is according to the will of God produces a repentance without regret, leading to salvation, but the sorrow of the world produces death.

Heavenly Father, we thank You that repentance leading to reconciliation is available to us. You are the Author of righteousness, unity, and peace. We thank You, Father, for godly sorrow that leads to repentance. Lead our hearts deeper into this godly sorrow that we can be rightly related with You and with others around us. Father, guard our hearts and minds from worldly sorrow. We want to walk closely in Your ways and truth and not be led astray in worldly wisdom or sorrow. Give us eyes to see and hearts to understand the difference and a quick willingness to repent as You lead.

Week 5: Intercession

SCRIPTURE

Ephesians 6:12, NASB (Participant Book, pg 28)

For our struggle is not against flesh and blood, but against the rulers, against the powers, against the world forces of this darkness, against the spiritual forces of wickedness in the heavenly places.

This verse is an important verse in the middle of a passage of Scripture that speaks of Christian warfare and being prepared for those battles.

In what ways is engaging in racial reconciliation a spiritual war?

TERMINOLOGY

"Intercession"

Consider this quote from Andrew Murray's *With Christ in the School of Prayer*:

There are two sorts of prayer: personal and intercessory. The latter ordinarily occupies the lesser part of our time and energy. This should not be. Christ has opened the school of prayer especially to train intercessors for the great work of bringing down, by their faith and prayer, the blessings of His work and love to the world. There can be no deep growth in prayer unless this is our aim. A child may ask its father to provide only what it needs for itself. But this child soon learns to say "Give some for my sister, too."[2]

Read Ezekiel 22:23-31 (Participant Book, pg 25)

This passage is admittedly full of doom and gloom and hard things. But the question stands: *"So I sought for a man among them who would make a wall, and stand in the gap before Me on behalf of the land"* (verse 30). Are we willing to be such people?

---

[2] Andrew Murray, *With Christ in the School of Prayer* (Springdale, PA: Whitaker House, 1981), 32.

How would you describe prayers of intercession? What does standing in the gap mean? How do we make a "wall" through prayer?

PRAYER

This week, we would like to take some time to actually utilize what Scripture teaches about intercession. We want to take some time today to put our faith into practice and pray together.

We will use Scripture, the inspired Word of God, to help lead us in our prayers. This helps us to know we are praying according to the will of God and to help keep our minds and hearts focused on the prayer at hand.

We have several verses typed, printed, and available to you. (Leaders, please prepare these ahead of time.) Please select a passage of Scripture, read it, think on it, and look for key words and ideas. We will sit in silence for a few moments as we each take a minute to ponder the Scriptures. In that moment, ask the Holy Spirit to help you pray. Then as the Lord prompts, read aloud the verse you are praying from and continue on in your own out-loud prayer from there.

This may feel awkward to some of you, but we encourage you to press past your feelings of insecurity and be bold in coming before the Lord. While you are waiting to pray, do the hard work of keeping your mind and heart engaged with the prayers of others.

(This first verse is for the leader to read and pray to open the time of prayer.)
Romans 8:26-27, NASB
In the same way the Spirit also helps our weakness; for we do not know how to pray as we should, but the Spirit Himself intercedes for us with groanings too deep for words; and He who searches the hearts knows what the mind of the Spirit is, because He intercedes for the saints according to the will of God.

John 17:20-23
I do not pray for these alone, but also for those who will believe in Me through their word that they all may be one, as You, Father, are in Me, and I in You; that they also may be one in Us, that the world may believe that You sent Me. And the glory which You gave Me I have given them, that they may be one just as We are one: I in them, and You in Me; that they may be made perfect in one, and that the world may know that You have sent Me, and have loved them as You have loved Me.

Zephaniah 2:1-3
Gather yourselves together, yes, gather together, O undesirable nation, before the decree is issued, or the day passes like chaff, before the Lord's fierce anger comes upon you! Seek the Lord, all you meek of the earth, who have upheld His justice. Seek righteousness, seek humility. It may be that you will be hidden in the day of the Lord's anger.

Ephesians 6:12, NASB
For our struggle is not against flesh and blood, but against the rulers, against the powers, against the world forces of this darkness, against the spiritual forces of wickedness in the heavenly places.

Micah 6:8, NIV
He has shown you, O man, what is good. And what does the Lord require of you? To act justly and to love mercy and to walk humbly with your God.

Hosea 10:12
Sow for yourselves righteousness; reap for mercy; break up your fallow ground, for it is time to seek the Lord, till He comes and rains righteousness on you.

James 3:13-18
Who is wise and understanding among you? Let him show by good conduct that his works are done in the meekness of wisdom. But if you have bitter envy and self-seeking in your hearts, do not boast and lie against the truth. This wisdom does not descend from above, but is earthly, sensual, demonic. For where envy and self-seeking exist, confusion and every evil thing are there. But the wisdom that is from above is first pure, then peaceable, gentle, willing to yield, full of mercy and good fruits, without partiality and without hypocrisy. Now the fruit of righteousness is sown in peace by those who make peace.

Ephesians 5:15-16, NIV
Be very careful, then, how you live--not as unwise but as wise, making the most of every opportunity, because the days are evil.

Proverbs 10:12,19
Hatred stirs up strife, but love covers all sins...In the multitude of words sin is not lacking, but he who restrains his lips is wise.

Psalm 51:1-4,17
Have mercy upon me, O God, according to Your lovingkindness;
According to the multitude of your tender mercies, blot out my transgressions,
Wash me thoroughly from my iniquity, and cleanse me from my sin.
For I acknowledge my transgressions, and my sin is always before me.
Against You, You only, have I sinned, and done this evil in Your sight
That You may be found just when You speak, and blameless when You judge...
The sacrifices of the Lord are a broken spirit, a broken and contrite heart--
These O God, You will not despise.

Psalm 72:3, ERV
Let there be peace and justice throughout the land, known on every
mountain and hill.

Ephesians 4:1-6
I, therefore, the prisoner of the Lord, beseech you to walk worthy of the calling with
which you were called, with all lowliness and gentleness, with longsuffering,
bearing with one another in love, endeavoring to keep the unity of the Spirit in the
bond of peace. There is one body and one Spirit, just as you were called in one
hope of your calling; one Lord, one faith, one baptism; one God and Father of all,
who is above all, and through all, and in you all.

Titus 3:1-5
Remind them...to speak evil of no one, to be peaceable, gentle, showing all
humility to all men. For we ourselves were also once foolish, disobedient,
deceived, serving various lusts and pleasures, living in malice and envy, hateful and
hating one another. But when the kindness and the love of God our Savior toward
man appeared...according to His mercy He saved us, through the washing of
regeneration and renewing of the Holy Spirit...

Colossians 3:8-11
But now you yourselves are to put off all these: anger, wrath, malice, blasphemy,
filthy language out of your mouth. Do not lie to one another, since you have put off
the old man with his deeds, and have put on the new man who is renewed in
knowledge according to the image of Him who created him, where there is neither
Greek nor Jew, circumcised nor uncircumcised, barbarian, Scythian, slave nor free,
but Christ is all and in all.

2 Corinthians 13:11, NIV
Strive for full restoration, encourage one another, be of one mind, live in peace.
And the God of love and peace will be with you.

NOTE: Feel free to add other verses you have found in your own personal study and prayer times. There is also a helpful prayer resource with suggested verses and corresponding prayer topics at: https://www.southeastchristian.org/18daysofprayer

Week 6: Seek Justice

SCRIPTURE

Micah 6:8, NASB (Participant Book, pg 34)
He has told you, O man, what is good;
And what does the Lord require of you
But to do justice, to love kindness,
And to walk humbly with your God?

For those of you that have been in the church for a while, this verse is likely familiar. It is often memorized and appears on Christian paraphernalia. But for the sake of our study, let's talk through what this verse is saying.

"He has told you, O man, what is good" - who is "He"? And what has He told us?

This verse names three things that are good and required by the Lord. Name those three things.

Describe what doing justice, loving kindness, and walking humbly with your God look like in everyday life.

HISTORY

We want to present a both/and kind of thought here. As we progress in our understanding of racial reconciliation and justice, we want to acknowledge that changes have taken place in our nation. Certain acts of justice have been enacted. However, there is still work to be done. Let's look at some moments that have brought about positive change for people of color, while also recognizing that those changes have not instituted full justice. (Leader, take some time to familiarize yourself with the topics and organizations mentioned below.)

Ways that racial justice has been sought:
• Emancipation Proclamation
• Civil Rights movement; MLK, Black Panthers
    • Voting Rights Act 1965
    • Desegregation
• Affirmative Action

Highlight the following as organizations working toward racial justice from a Biblical perspective. If you as the leader are not familiar with these organizations, we highly recommend exploring these organizations ahead of time in order for you to accurately share the vision of each:

• Equal Justice Initiative
• Civil Righteousness
• OneRace

• ANDcampaign
• Be the Bridge

DISCUSSION QUESTIONS

Let's define justice again and discuss its meaning. In this week's chapter (Participant Book, pg 32), we used a quote from *False Justice* to define it:

> *Most people think of justice only as punitive, but justice is far more than that. God's justice is about wholeness and divine order of everything that He has created. We usually think of justice operating within the social sphere and legal realm; however, God's justice encompasses every sphere, both spiritual and natural, including the environment, our homes, our workplaces, governments, friendships, and our inner life. At its core, justice is about everything being made whole.*[3]

• What do you think about this quote?

• In what ways can followers of Jesus focus on their own personal relationship with the Lord, or even reaching the lost, without demonstrating the love and Gospel of Christ to the world around them?

• How has this affected racial relationships in the church and our communities?

• What are some next step ideas that you individually, or we as a group, can take to bring the Gospel, holistically, to the various spheres we have access to?

---

[3] Stuart Greaves, *False Justice: Unveiling the Truth about Social Justice* (Shippensburg, PA: Destiny Image Publishers, 2012), 31.

PRAYER

Isaiah 26:8b-9

O Lord, we have waited for You; The desire of our soul is for Your name and for the remembrance of You. With my soul I have desired You in the night. Yes, by my spirit within me I will seek You early; For when Your judgments are in the earth, the inhabitants of the world will learn righteousness.

Oh, Lord, I repeat these words - we have waited for You. The desire of our souls is for Your name and the remembrance of You to be magnified and glorified in the world. We want Your church to be a credible witness in the earth, for racial divides to be broken down and thus for the world to see the love and power of the cross. As Your followers, Lord, help us to show the truth of Your judgments and right living to those around us. May our love and care for the others around us display the truth of Your heart for a unified and diverse church.

Week 7: Table

SCRIPTURE

1 Peter 1:22-23, 2:1-5

Since you have purified your souls in obeying the truth through the Spirit in sincere love of the brethren, love one another fervently with a pure heart, having been born again, not of corruptible seed but incorruptible, through the word of God which lives and abides forever...Therefore, laying aside all malice, all deceit, hypocrisy, envy, and all evil speaking, as newborn babes, desire the pure milk of the word that you may grow thereby if indeed you have tasted that the Lord is gracious. Coming to Him as to a living stone, rejected indeed by men, but chosen by God and precious, you also, as living stones, are being built up a spiritual house, a holy priesthood, to offer up spiritual sacrifices acceptable to God through Jesus Christ.

This passage of Scripture is jam packed with ideas and things to consider. To start, let's just call out the main ideas this passage speaks about.

Now that we have named the spiritual principles found in this passage, let's talk about how and what those concepts look like fleshed out practically.

• What does obeying the truth through the Spirit in sincere love of the brethren or loving one another with a pure heart look like?

• How do you lay aside malice or deceit or envy or hypocrisy?

• What does it look like to desire the pure milk of the word?

And lastly, let's just imagine the future for a moment. This passage tells us that we are living stones that will be used to build a spiritual house. Imagine this spiritual house for just a minute. Do you imagine a building that has one white side and one black side? One Asian side? Or do you imagine a house with bricks that blend together in color and shade making a beautifully designed exterior?

Our Father is a Master Builder. He desires greatly to build a spiritual house that reflects His diversity and therefore His glory. Brick laying beside brick. Person built beside person. Beside, below, and above. Masterfully displaying His beautiful Bride.

HISTORY

Sharing a meal and sitting at a table together means that we will be getting up close and personal with our lives, thoughts, and personal stories. To date, we have discussed bits of our national history, Biblical history, and Church history. We have even touched on some of our current racial context in America. Today, let's take a look at our own family history. Think back to your grandparents, your parents, your own life. What memories or stories can you think of that relate to racial reconciliation? Do you have memories or stories of you or your family hindering the equal treatment of all people regardless of the color of their skin? Do you have memories or stories of you or your family reaching across racial divides?

These can be super sensitive questions to ask and possibly even more difficult to answer. There are stories and memories on all sides of the discussion that apply. If you are willing, we encourage you to speak out the good, the bad, and the ugly. Confession is part of seeing rightly. Repentance, where necessary, brings forgiveness and healing. And as Acts 3:19 says, *"Repent therefore and be converted, that your sins may be blotted out, so that times of refreshing may come from the presence of the Lord."*

DISCUSSION QUESTIONS

• What are three different kinds of tables we can gather around as brothers and sisters in Christ? (Participant Book, pg 39-40)

- Literal dining room table
- Metaphorical table of bringing other voices into spaces and conversations around you, particularly in decision-making contexts
- Implied table of meetings and gatherings and the work of building relationships even if a literal meal or social event is not feasible

• What are some ways you can "set a table" and build relationships across racial or ethnic lines?

This video is a Facebook link of a video recording of Jonathan Tremain Thomas of Civil Righteous discussing what the concept of "coming to the table" looks like. The video is an hour long and therefore too long to share in class, but it may be a good resource to email out to your group for them to watch/listen to on their own time. https://fb.watch/2Tb-OwvZAs/

PRAYER

....

Hebrews 6:10-12, 19-20

For God is not unjust to forget your work and labor of love which you have shown toward His name, in that you have ministered to the saints, and do minister. And we desire that each one of you show the same diligence to the full assurance of hope until the end, that you do not become sluggish, but imitate those who through faith and patience inherit the promises….This hope we have as an anchor of the soul, both sure and steadfast, and which enters the Presence behind the veil, where the forerunner has entered for us, even Jesus, having become High Priest forever according to the order of Melchizedek.

Holy Father, thank You. Thank you that You do not forget the work and the labor of love that we have done in this room the past several weeks. You see and hear and move in us and through us. As we go from this place, help us to be diligent in the truth we have learned. Enable us to push off sluggishness and instead continue working with patience and faith towards the unified Bride You are creating. Thank You, Father, for hope. Thank You that You provided an anchor of hope in Jesus, that we can continue faithfully in truth and love, loving and serving specifically across racial barriers in order for You to be glorified in the earth.

Week 8: Hope

SCRIPTURE

Romans 8:18-25, NASB (Participant Book, pg 43)

For I consider that the sufferings of this present time are not worthy to be compared with the glory that is to be revealed to us. For the anxious longing of the creation waits eagerly for the revealing of the sons of God. For the creation was subjected to futility, not willingly, but because of Him who subjected it, in hope that the creation itself also will be set free from its slavery to corruption into the freedom of the glory of the children of God. For we know that the whole creation groans and suffers the pains of childbirth together until now. And not only this, but also we ourselves, having the first fruits of the Spirit, even we ourselves groan within ourselves, waiting eagerly for our adoption as sons, the redemption of our body. For in hope we have been saved, but hope that is seen is not hope; for who hopes for what he already sees? But if we hope for what we do not see, with perseverance we wait eagerly for it.

As we wrap up our study together, let's look at what this passage has to say about hope.

- What tone or emotion would you characterize this passage with?

- What is the context of this passage? What is happening in "this present age" as mentioned in verse 18?

- What was creation subjected to?

- Who subjected it?

- What purpose was it subjected for?

- In what ways does this verse describe hope?

HISTORY

With the exception of our Intercession week, we have tackled various pieces of the history of racism in our nation. As we close out this study, we don't want to leave our eyes looking behind, only being taillights on this problem. Instead we want to look forward. We want to cultivate a dream and a hope. We want to be the headlights illuminating the path forward.

The Action recommendation in the Participant Book (pg 46) this week was:

Take some time this week to specifically thank the Lord for what you have learned through this study, what relationships you have formed, and what you have been challenged with. Take some time to write down your thoughts and ideas for next steps and practical ways you can continue the journey and anything else the Lord puts on your heart. Dream big! Share your ideas with a friend and keep the paper somewhere it can serve as a reminder and source of accountability for you.

If you have done this already, or if you have not, let's take a few minutes now to share things we have learned, areas we want to grow in, and dreams and hopes for our future.

DISCUSSION QUESTIONS

- From the Participant Book (pg 43), what do the letters of HOPE represent?
- Discuss as a group the importance of and the challenges in Humility, Obedience, Patience, and Endurance as they pertain to hope.

PRAYER

Romans 15:13, NASB (Participant Book, pg 42)
Now may the God of hope fill you with all joy and peace in believing, so that you will abound in hope by the power of the Holy Spirit.

Gracious Father, You have been so good and kind to speak to our minds and hearts during the time of this study. Going from these rooms and out in our homes, our churches, and our neighborhoods we need the filling of Your hope. You are the God of hope, You fill us with joy and peace in believing. And as such we are able to walk in our spheres and places of influence by the power of the Holy Spirit. Lord, we thank You that You enable us to walk in truth, righteousness, and love. Fill us anew today with the power of Your Spirit to love equally, deeply, and in hope of a future more closely aligned with Your Kingdom in the earth.